D0622540

Snap books ® Babysitter's Backpack

You're HiRED!

Business Basics

Every

BABYSITTER

Needs to Know

by Rebecca Rissman

Consultant:
Lyn Horning
Assistant Director, Better Kid Care
Penn State University
University Park, Pennsylvania

CAPSTONE PRESS
a capstone imprint

Snap Books are published by Capstone Press,
1710 Roe Crest Drive, North Mankato, Minnesota 56003
www.capstonepub.com

Library of Congress Cataloging-in-Publication Data
Rissman, Rebecca.
  You're hired! : business basics every babysitter needs to know / by Rebecca Rissman.
    pages cm. — (Babysitter's backpack)
  Includes index.
  ISBN 978-1-4914-0766-0 (library binding) — ISBN 978-1-4914-0770-7 (eBook pdf)
1. Babysitters—Juvenile literature. 2. Vocational guidance—Juvenile literature. I. Title. II.
Title: You are hired.
  HQ769.R5727 2015
  649'.10248—dc23
                            2014006973

Editorial Credits
Abby Colich, editor; Juliette Peters, designer; Tracy Cummins, media researcher;
Laura Manthe, production specialist

Photo Credits
Capstone Press: Karon Dubke, 1 Bottom Right, 1 Bottom Left, 2 Bottom Left, 2 Bottom Right, 4, 9 Top, 10, 13 Top, 14 Top, 16 Top Left, 18, 20, 21 Top, 22, 23, 26 Bottom; iStockphotos: Kali Nine LLC, 8, Mlenny, 12, skynesher, 24; Shutterstock: Denis Cristo, Cover, Design Element, Elena Stepanova, 15 Bottom, 16 Bottom Right, Forestpath, 27 Top, lightpoet, 6, Monkey Business Images, 7, Natykach Nataliia, 28 Top, Design Element, Sean Locke Photography, 25, Stephanie Barbary, 5 Top, Steve Cukrov, 11, Veerachai Viteeman, Design Element

Printed in the United States of America in North Mankato, Minnesota.
032014   008087CGF14

Page 4

Page 14

Table of Contents

Start Your Own Business

Looking to make some extra money? You might think you're too young to start your own business. Think again! Many young people become entrepreneurs by starting small businesses, such as neighborhood car washes, lemonade stands, or dog-walking services.

If you enjoy caring for children, you could start your own babysitting business. Once you learn the basics, your schedule could be full of babysitting jobs and your piggy bank full of spending money.

Got the Time?

Starting your own business is exciting and fun. But first make sure you will have time for it. If you are already very busy with homework, wait until the summer to open your business.

If you are involved in school activities, such as band or a sports team, remember to make time for these. Dedicate one or two days a week to these activities, and never schedule babysitting jobs on those days.

Also make sure you have your parents' permission to babysit. Discuss with them how much you plan on babysitting and if they will need to drive you to any jobs.

What Should You Do quiz questions throughout will help you figure out if you're ready to be a great babysitter. You can look up the answers on page 29.

First Thing First

Before you start any business, you'll need some training. You wouldn't open a bakery without learning how to bake cookies. And you wouldn't want to start babysitting without learning some important child-care skills first.

Go to your local Red Cross or community center to enroll in a first aid course. These classes will teach you what to do during a medical emergency. You'll learn how to respond if a child begins choking or becomes unconscious. It will also teach you how to treat small injuries such as scrapes and bruises.

Next, enroll in a babysitter training class at a local school or church. If you can't find one near you, ask a parent or trusted adult to help you find one online. The Red Cross website offers great options. A babysitter training class will teach you skills and tips to be a safe babysitter and smart businessperson. You will learn important child care and safety rules. It will also teach you how to organize your schedule, act professionally, and build a strong business.

Getting Experience

Do you have experience caring for children? If your answer is no, don't worry. Ask neighbors or family friends about volunteer babysitting for them while they're home. If you are nervous, ask one or both parents to stay in the same room with you and the children. As you get more comfortable, they can relax in other parts of the house while you care for their children. This is a great way to learn about babysitting because you can ask the parents for any help or advice you need. The parents will enjoy the free child care too!

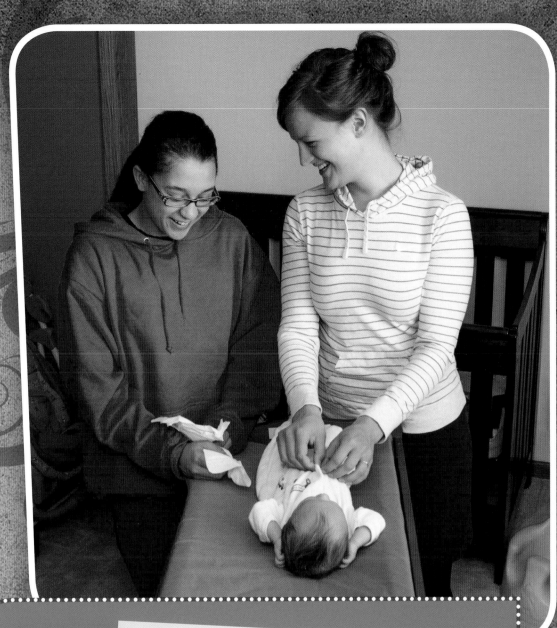

What Should You Do?

You are interested in learning how to care for babies. You hear from your friends at school that your neighbors have a newborn. What should you do?

A Ask your neighbors if you can come over and help her care for the baby free of charge while they are home.

B Take a class on infant care.

C Ask a trusted adult for tips on caring for babies.

D All of the above.

9

CHAPTER 2

Be a Business Pro

Once you've learned how to safely care for children, it's time to think about how you'll run your babysitting business.

Money Matters

One of the first things to decide is your rate, or how much money you will charge per hour. Ask friends who babysit about their rates. Do they charge extra for more than one child? Do they charge more to work on the weekends or late at night? If so, how much? Also ask your parents, neighbors, or other trusted adults with children how much they pay their babysitters. Try to set a rate that is comparable to what your friends and other babysitters charge.

Some customers might want to pay a flat rate. This means they will pay you the same amount for every babysitting job. Make sure you discuss this with them before accepting a job.

Once you have decided on your rate, stick with it. Try not to charge different customers different rates. It will be confusing, and some customers might be upset if they learn they are paying more than others.

Discuss with customers ahead of time if they will be paying you with cash or a check. If you don't already have a bank account, you may want to ask a parent to help you get one started.

Tracking Your Earnings

Keep your finances organized. A good way to do this is to keep a money log on your computer or in a notebook. After each job write down the date you babysat, who you worked for, how much you charged per hour, and if you got a tip.

Date	Family	Rate per hour	Number of hours	Tip
Nov. 3	Johnsons	$8	5	$5
Dec. 5	Patels	Flat fee: $30	3	none

Earning Money

What will you do with all the money you make? It's a good idea to plan how you will spend your money. Try making a pie chart showing the percent you hope to save, spend, and put back into your business.

30%
spending money

5%
babysitting supplies

65%
savings

What Should You Do?

You agree to babysit one child and explain your single-child rate. But when you arrive, the parents tell you you'll be watching three children instead of one. What should you do?

A Tell them you agreed to babysit one child, not three. Go back home.

B Agree but explain that you will need to charge extra for the other children. You will also need to confirm that the other children's parents know that you are babysitting.

C Say nothing about the additional children. You don't want to be rude.

D Tell them you will stay only if the other children leave.

Become a Master of Marketing

All successful businesses need customers. You might already have a few customers. But you can take your business to the next level with some simple marketing.

A great way to market yourself is to make flyers and business cards. These are like small advertisements for your business. Make colorful flyers and hand them out to your neighbors, teachers, and family friends. Make sure to include your rate, qualifications, and the training courses you have taken. Also include the times you are available to work.

Do you have friends who regularly babysit? Ask if you can contact their customers about being a backup babysitter when your friends are unavailable.

Remember!

Always be safe. Never give anything with your contact information to strangers. Never post your flyers in public places.

Bella's Babysitting Business

QUALIFICATIONS:

Red Cross certified

Babysitter Training Course certified

First Aid certified

AVAILABILITY:

Monday through Thursday,
4:00 p.m.–8:00 p.m.

RATE:

$8 per hour for one child
plus $1 per hour for every additional child

Contact Information: 555-8910
BellaBabysits@teenemail.com

Bella's
Babysitting Business

Monday–Thursday
4:00 p.m.–8:00 p.m.

$8 per hour for one child
plus $1 per hour for every additional child

Business Cards

Business cards are small pieces of paper that tell people your name, your business, and how you can be reached. They don't contain as much information as a flyer, but they are easy to carry in your pocket or wallet.

To make your own business cards, cut thick paper into small rectangles. Then write your business name on one side and your name and contact information on the other side. Keep five to 10 business cards with you at all times. You never know when a neighbor or family friend will be looking for a new babysitter.

Get References

References are people who can recommend you as a babysitter to others. When you work for a family, ask the parents if they would be a reference for you.

Make a Résumé

A résumé is an important tool for any businessperson. It is a short summary of you, your experience, and your interests. You can give your résumé to people you hope to babysit for.

Use this template to create your own résumé!

Your Name

your address	your phone number
city, state	your e-mail address
zip code	

Education

your school   your grade level

Training

any courses you have taken and a brief description of each

Babysitting Experience

family name   date
brief description of your babysitting duties

family name   date
brief description of your babysitting duties

Hobbies

any hobbies or special interests you have

References

name   phone number   relationship to you
name   phone number   relationship to you

CHAPTER 3

The Right Customers

When a parent or guardian responds to your flyer, arrange to meet him or her for an interview. This is a short meeting where you can ask questions and get to know the family. Ask a trusted adult or older sibling to go with you.

Be Choosy

Just as customers choose their babysitters, you can choose your customers. Make sure that you feel comfortable with the family during your interview. Does the family have a newborn, a child with special needs, or more children than you can comfortably care for? Think about what you're ready and able to handle. If you feel uncomfortable with the parents or children, don't take any babysitting jobs from the family.

If the customer doesn't live close to you, talk about how you will get to and from their home. Make sure you have a safe and reliable ride for every babysitting job you accept. If you live close enough to walk, always ask a trusted adult to walk with you.

Some questions to ask during your interview are:

- How many children do you have? How old are they?
- Do any of your children have special needs or illnesses?
- What days and times will you need a babysitter?
- Do you have pets? If so, is the babysitter expected to care for them?
- Will you need a babysitter on a regular basis or just for special occasions?

Making the Right Impression

It's important to make a good impression during your interview. Do your best to show that you are a great babysitter who is responsible and caring. Wear clean and appropriate clothing. And remember to bring your résumé! The family will want to ask you questions too. Be prepared to answer these or similar questions.

- How long have you been a babysitter?
- How many families do you babysit for?
- What is your favorite thing about babysitting?
- What types of activities would you do with my children?
- Have you ever had an emergency while babysitting? If so, what did you do?

What Should You Do?

You get an e-mail from someone who says they saw one of your babysitting flyers. They want you to babysit right now. You've never met them, but they offer you more than twice your rate. What should you do?

A Tell the customer that before you work for a stranger, you always arrange a meeting that includes your parent or other trusted adult. Ask if they would like to arrange a meeting.

B Go ahead! It's going to be a big payday!

C Agree to the job, but tell a friend where you're going before you leave.

D Call the police. This sounds dangerous.

Grow Your Business

The best way to get new customers is to do a great job for the families you already work for. When you impress parents with your child care skills and professionalism, they are more likely to recommend you to others.

Being Professional

Always try to do your very best when you babysit. Treat every job as though it is the most important babysitting job ever. Acting in a professional manner shows that you take your job seriously. Here are some professional practices to follow:

- Before you accept a job, make sure you're available. Also get your parents' permission.
- Let the family know if you have a curfew.
- Only cancel a babysitting job if there is an emergency or you are sick. Let the family know as soon as possible.
- Arrive on time and be ready to work.
- Follow the parents' instructions and house rules.
- Clean up after yourself and any messes the children make while under your care.
- Do not use your cell phone, smoke, use drugs or alcohol, invite friends over, or look through the family's belongings.

Babysit for a Group

After you have gotten comfortable babysitting for one family at a time, you can grow your business by babysitting for more than one family at once. Look for chances to provide child care at neighborhood picnics, church gatherings, or parties. These events are a great way to meet new families and show them your babysitting skills. Remember, never accept a babysitting job that you are not comfortable with. Always make sure you can do a good job caring for every single child.

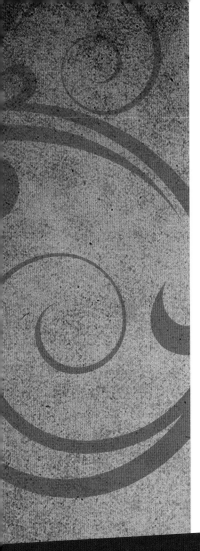

Keeping It Straight

Once word gets out about your amazing babysitting business, you can expect to hear from more families. It's important to stay organized so that you know when you have booked jobs and when you are available to work. Create a calendar to help you keep everything straight.

Use a calendar to organize your schedule. You can set an alert on your phone or computer, or hang a paper calendar in your room.

Include the following details for each job in your calendar:

- family's address and phone number
- name of family and names and ages of their children
- work hours
- how you will get there and back

THURSDAY	FRIDAY	SATURDAY
Babysit at the Schneiders 34 Oaklane Dr. 555-5309 Children: Suzette (age 5), Dylan (age 2), and Nolan (6 months) Time: 4:00–7:00 p.m. Transportation: Mr. Schneider will pick me up and drop me off **1**	Babysit at the Dells 9867 Main Ave. 555-8910 Children: Matilda (age 10) and John (age 4) Time: 5:00–7:30 p.m. Transportation: Mom will drive me there and back **2**	Babysit at the Changs 5412 Waverly Pl. 555-7902 Children: Allison (age 7) and Chloe (age 4) Time: 1:00–4:00 p.m. Transportation: I will ride my bike **3**

Remember!

Send thank-you notes to families after you babysit for them for the first time. This tells them that you enjoyed spending time with their children. It will also let them know that you are interested in working for them in the future.

Take Care of Yourself

Have fun. Babysitting is a job, but you should enjoy it. Try not to take on too many babysitting jobs. Save some time for yourself. If you work too often, you might find yourself falling behind on homework, feeling stressed, or missing your friends.

What Should You Do?

You've got a big violin recital in two days, and you need to practice. A neighbor calls and asks if you can babysit tomorrow night for three hours. What should you do?

A Accept the job. You can practice after you get home from babysitting, even if it makes you tired.

B Accept the job and plan to bring your violin. You can practice while the kids play.

C Politely turn the job down. You need to practice the violin and rest before the recital.

D Tell the neighbor you'll think about it and quickly hang up the phone. You don't have time for this!

Babysitting Briefcase

You might have seen an adult carrying a briefcase to work. Why not make your own babysitting briefcase to bring along with you on your jobs? Find an old backpack or bag and fill it with items such as these:

- babysitting journal—write down any special notes about the children you babysit, such as favorite foods and bedtime rules so you will be prepared for future jobs
- your planner or calendar
- small bills in case your customers need you to make change
- homework or a book to read after the kids go to bed
- crafts or activities to do with the children

Babysitting Checklist

Before you take your first babysitting job, make sure you do the following:

- learn CPR, take first aid training, and complete a basic babysitting skills course
- decide on your hourly rate
- interview the customer
- confirm details about how you are getting to and from your job
- get your parents' permission, and tell them where you are working and when you will be home

What Should You Do?
Quiz Answers

page 9

D All of the above.

Make sure you know how to feed, diaper, and care for infants before you babysit one. Ask an adult for tips and take a babysitting course if you can. Volunteer babysitting an infant is also a great way to learn about baby care.

page 13

B Agree, but explain that you will need to charge extra for the other children. You will also need to confirm that the other children's parents know that you are babysitting.

Babysitting more than one child is more work. Be sure you get paid for your work. Call the parents of the other children to confirm they know you are babysitting. Be sure to ask if their children have any special issues you need to be aware of.

page 21

A Tell the customer that before you work for a stranger, you always arrange a meeting that includes your parent or other trusted adult. Ask if they would like to arrange a meeting.

Never accept a job from a stranger without first scheduling an interview. Make sure that each babysitting job you accept is safe.

page 27

D Politely turn the job down. You need to practice the violin and rest before the recital.

Your babysitting jobs should not take away from your homework or extracurricular activities. You also shouldn't schedule so many babysitting jobs that you don't have any time for yourself.

Glossary

enroll (in-ROLL)—to sign up to take a class or course

entrepreneur (ON-truh-pruh-new-IHR)—a person who starts his or her own business

interview (IN-tur-vyoo)—to ask someone questions to find out more about something

marketing (MAR-ke-ting)—advertising or raising awareness of a service

qualification (KWAHL-uh-fi-kay-shun)—skills or special training

rate (RAYT)—the amount of money someone charges

unconscious (uhn-KON-shuhss)—not awake; not able to see, feel, or think

volunteer (vol-uhn-TIHR)—to work without pay

Read More

American Red Cross. *American Red Cross Babysitter's Training Handbook.* Yardley, Penn.: Staywell, 2008.

Babysitting Secrets: Everything You Need to Have a Successful Babysitting Business. San Francisco: Chronicle Books, 2012.

Bondy, Halley. *Don't Sit on the Baby!: The Ultimate Guide to Sane, Skilled, and Safe Babysitting.* San Francisco: Zest Books, 2012.

Internet Sites

FactHound offers a safe, fun way to find Internet sites related to this book. All of the sites on FactHound have been researched by our staff.

Here's all you do:

Visit *www.facthound.com*

Type in this code: 9781491407660

Check out projects, games and lots more at
www.capstonekids.com

Index